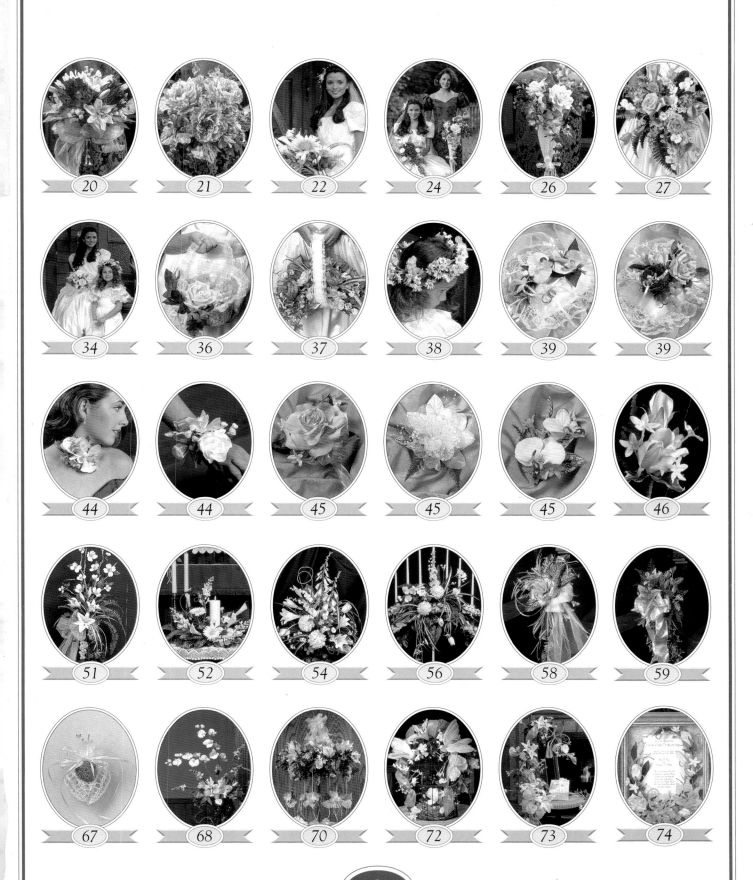

20

21

22

24

26

27

34

36

37

38

39

39

44

44

45

45

45

46

51

52

54

56

58

59

67

68

70

72

73

74

Dear Bride To Be,

Flowers speak the language of love. They help set the mood of your wedding day and become part of your cherished memories. You want your flowers to be beautiful, to be professional looking and to reflect your personal style. They must be perfect for your wedding day.

You may be a beginner or may have never considered yourself creative enough to do wedding flowers. This book has been designed to guide you through the fundamentals. It will help you plan, choose designs and flowers to create arrangements that let your personality shine through. The classic designs shown in each project lend themselves to an informal garden wedding as well as a traditional church wedding.

The designer, Michelle Ta, has extensive training and experience in floral design, interior design and fine art. Using her experience as a teacher, she has put together easy-to-follow instructions so you can create professional floral arrangements. You, your family and friends can keep the arrangements long after the wedding is over. They will become treasured mementos that you patiently made with your own hands.

Planning Your Flowers

The colors you choose along with the styles of gowns and places for the ceremony and reception will all work together to create your unique wedding. To plan the flowers, it will be important to know the style and colors of the gowns so you can pick appropriate bouquets and flowers. For the ceremony and reception, you'll need to know a variety of things to decide how many and what type of arrangements to make. Each place will have its own flavor and decorating needs.

As you are choosing the locations, jot down all the decorating ideas you have. Verify with the person in charge that it will be all right to bring in and place the pieces where you want them.

Many locations will also have containers, stands, candle holders or props available to rent or to use. If they do not, check with your local florist to rent large items or a lot of the same items. Arches, standing baskets, and a variety of centerpiece containers are usually available. Some florists or specialty stores will even rent out live and silk plants to use on tables or around the room.

Here are a few questions you may want to ask:

- How is the place usually decorated for a wedding?

- Are there any pieces available to use or to rent?

- Are there any restrictions on size or placement of various arrangements?

- Are you allowed to use wire, tape or pins to attach bows and garlands?

- Can anything be hung on walls? How should you hang it?

- How will the room or area be set up on the day of the wedding?

- Can you have a copy of the floor plan?

- How much time is allowed before the ceremony and reception to get all the decorations set up?

Some other things to remember:

- Who is the person or people that will be setting up all the decorations?

- Does that person need to see the place in order to set them up correctly?

- Is there enough time allowed to have friends set up and be to the ceremony on time?

- Who will be in charge of removing the decorations after the wedding and returning any rental items?

Decorating can be as elaborate or simple as you choose. The locations you choose will determine most of what needs to be done, but the final picture is up to you.

By making your arrangements with silk flowers, you can have everything your heart desires and make them months in advance. They will still look freshly picked on the big day when you use quality, realistic silks.

Here are a few more time saving tips:

- If you are making a swag for the arch at the ceremony, remove it afterwards and lay it on the head table as the centerpiece.

- Bring the two altar arrangements from the ceremony and place them back to back on the buffet table. This makes a beautiful, round centerpiece. They could also be placed behind the food for a one sided buffet.

- Rent clear glass bowls and float a single fresh open rose, gardenia or floating candle in each one for the guest tables.

- Rent silk trees and string white lights through them to add a soft glow around the room.

- Decorate baskets or bowls with flowers and fill each one with wedding favors for table centerpieces.

- Float helium balloons on the ceiling above the dance floor. Leave long strings hanging and tie a few flowers into some of them.

- Add flowers to a branch wreath or garland base. Use the wreath on round tables with a candle in the center. For long tables, place a few candles along the center of the table and weave the garland through them.

- Have a professional make one centerpiece to your specifications. Using that as your guide, buy the flowers and supplies needed to copy it for all your guest tables.

After you've chosen the gowns and locations, it's time to choose your flowers.

Flower check list (page 7)

Photocopy the list on the next page to plan how many pieces you will need.

On the list, write in the names of all the people. Be sure to include any family and friends that do not have a category. This will ensure that no one is forgotten. The names can also be put on the arrangements once they are completed. Friends can then make sure each person receives the right piece on the day of the wedding.

Under the ceremony and reception categories, write in the general location and quantity of each piece. This will help the person decorating remember what they should have and where they should go.

As you choose an arrangement for each person and place, write the page number on the list next to their name or the location. This will help you create a complete shopping list of flowers and supplies before you head to the store. Use the back of the photocopy to list the amount and types of flowers you'll need. Be sure to include any supplies and list rental items you need to reserve.

Flower Check List

NUMBER OF ARRANGEMENTS		
FOR PEOPLE:	**FOR CEREMONY:**	**FOR RECEPTION:**
Bride:	Altar arrangement:	Cake:
Maid of Honor:	Candelabras:	Head table:
Bridesmaids:	Unity candle:	Guest tables:
Flower girl:	Arch or Gazebo:	Guest book:
Groom:	Entry:	Buffet:
Best man:	Kneeling bench:	Entry:
Groomsmen:	Pew bows:	Additional:
Ring bearer:	Aisle:	
Ushers:	Additional Decorations:	
Mothers:		
Fathers:		
Grandmothers:		
Grandfathers:		
Additional family:		
Friends/Helpers:		

FINDING FLOWER SUBSTITUTIONS

The colors of your flowers are the most important and your wedding will have your own special colors. As the styles of flowers change with each season, you will be able to pick out a unique assortment that fits your personal taste.

The designs in this book are your foundation for creating beautiful, professional arrangements in your own colors and flower choices. Check the materials list of each project to see how many flowers you will need and what type they should be.

Follow this easy guide to substitute the types of flowers used in each project:

Line Flowers:

Line flowers are used to create the overall shape of each arrangement. They are usually long, straight stems of single flowers. Greenery can also be used to create the line. Remember, stems with a spray of flowers and bushes can be cut apart into single stems.

Focal Flowers:

Focal flowers can also be called primary flowers. They become the center or the main focal point of the arrangement. They are usually large single flowers, showy and bigger than the other flowers used in the same arrangement.

Filler Flowers:

Filler flowers are used to fill in the empty spaces throughout the arrangement. They bind all the flowers together to create a complete shape and finished look. They are usually the smallest flowers. Any shape of small, delicate flowers or greenery can be used. It's best to cut apart sprays and bushes so the filler can be spread out evenly throughout the arrangement.

TOOLS AND SUPPLIES

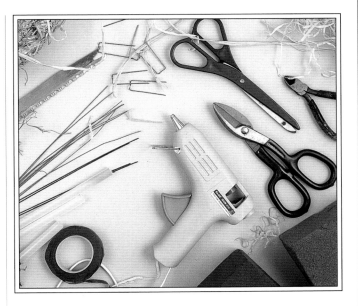

To make any of the projects, you will need some standard tools and supplies in addition to the project materials. The following is a list of the most commonly used in this book. Purchase or gather them together before you begin making the arrangements.

a. Wire cutters

b. Scissors

c. Glue gun/glue sticks (or pan melt)

d. Floral tape, stem wrap

e. Yard stick or ruler

f. Floral wires (various gauges from light #30 to heavy #16)

g. Wooden picks with attached wire

h. Floral foam, caged floral foam

i. Bridal bouquet holders

j. Bouquet stand or substitute

Bouquet holders come in different sizes and types. The sizes are the Jr., Standard and Extra Large. The purpose is to accommodate the amount of flowers and the weight of the bouquet. The two types are regular (the kind that absorbs water) and dry (the kind that will not absorb water). When using silk flowers, always use the dry foam. Regular foam may crumble or be too weak to hold heavy silk stems.

Bouquet stands hold the bouquet holder while you are creating the arrangement. Professionals use a stand with slots for the handle. The handle can be placed down from the top or into the side from the front. Placing the handle down allows the bride to carry the bouquet from the bottom using both hands. Placing it in the front allows her to carry the bouquet from the back using one hand.

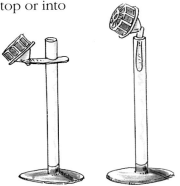

If you cannot use a stand, there are many substitutions. Anything that holds the handle, is heavy enough to support the weight on one side and leaves your hands free will work. A large bottle filled with sand is the easiest substitute. You can also fill a pot with sand and attach a sheet of Styrofoam to one side. The handle can then be inserted through the foam to hold it in place.

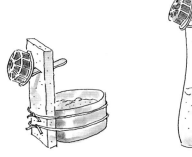

Caged floral foam is foam with a plastic case over it. The case is solid in back and has open spaces around the front and sides. There are many shapes and sizes. Primarily it is used for hanging arrangements such as swags for arches. The case acts as the container. It supports the weight of the flowers and keeps the foam from falling apart when it is hung. Many styles come with a handle, hanger or suction cup so it can be easily placed or held.

PREPARING THE FLOWERS

Before beginning each project, make sure you have all your tools, supplies and materials gathered together.

Remember these handy tips:

- It will help you concentrate if you pre-cut all the flower stems to the correct lengths before you start arranging them.

- Always measure from the tip of the flowers or greens, unless otherwise indicated.

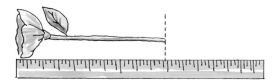

- If you have to cut in the middle of a line flower, remove some of the flowers above the cut line so it can be inserted easily into the foam.

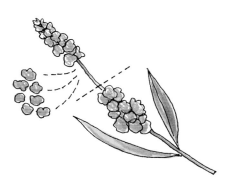

- If the flower is not long enough, wrap a wired wooden pick around the stem to add a few inches. To add a lot of length, tape a heavy floral wire or a discarded stem to the stem of the flower.

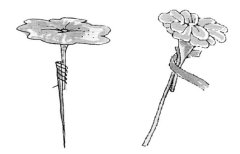

- Cut apart bushes or stems with multiple flowers into single stems. Add length if needed using the previous method.

- As you place the flowers into floral foam, add some hot glue to the stem. The glue will harden and keep the flowers exactly in place.

- If you need to move a glued flower after the arrangement is complete, simply cut the stem at the foam level.

- For a broken flower head or one that just can't keep its head on, place a dab of glue on the top of the stem and push the flower back down over it.

Corsage Techniques

Preparing the flowers

Pierce method:

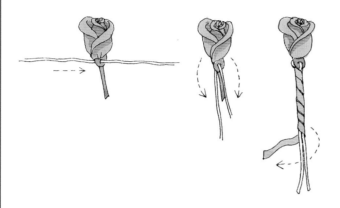

Hook method:

Bundle method:

Shortcuts For Silk Flowers

The wire stem of the flower and green can usually be utilized instead of rewiring and taping. If you need only one, two or three inches of stem, tape over it first and cut it to the desired length.

If you need the stem to be longer, lighter or more pliable, cut the stem below the flower to three or four inches and tape a floral wire over it.

Filler flowers and greens can be added to each flower with hot glue.

Making the Corsages

Single cluster: Add the filler and greens to the flower by wrapping the wire stems of each around the flower. Always add the filler first to surround the flower and the greens last to frame it in. Cut excess wire off after wrapping it around twice. This keeps the cluster from getting too heavy.

Adding clusters together: Make three to five single clusters. Wrap the stem of one around the next to form the corsage. A bow can be added at any point by wrapping its wire onto a cluster.

Hair pieces: The first step in a hair piece is to make a corsage.

For barrettes and combs: Use a separate floral wire to attach the completed corsage to the barrette. Wrap one end of the wire to the top of the barrette and tighten it. Lay the corsage on the barrette and wrap the wire tightly around both. Silk or dry corsages can also be hot glued on the barrette.

For wreaths, the bundle method is used. First, measure a separate floral wire or wires to fit the person's head.

Wrap that wire with stem wrap.

Second, prepare the flower bundles. As you finish each bundle, lay them over the head wire and wrap the stem around it. Tape each one in place, overlapping each bundle slightly. When the head wire is covered, bend it into a circle and connect the ends together with wire or a bow.

For Garlands: The same technique is used for garlands as for hair wreaths. First, measure a wire to the desired length. A much heavier gauge wire would be used for garlands than for hair wreaths. Cover this wire with stem wrap. Prepare the flower clusters using the bundle method. Each should be four to six inches long and fuller than the hair wreath bundles.

Add the flower bundles to the main wire the same way. Add bows to either end of the garland once it is complete. It will be pliable enough to bend to the desired form, and can be hung by the wires on the bows.

RIBBONS & BOWS

FLORAL BOW

1 Make a loop leaving the tail the desired length.

2 Continue making loops gradually increasing the size of the loops until the bow is full and you have enough ribbon left over to make the remaining tail.

3 Secure the center of the bow with floral wire.

4 Fan out the loops.

5 Cut the tails at an angle or in points to finish off the bow.

LOOPY BOW

1 Make a loop leaving the tail the desired length.

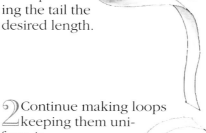

2 Continue making loops keeping them uniform in size until the bow is full and you have enough ribbon left over to make the remaining tail.

3 Secure the center of the bow with floral wire.

4 Fan out the loops.

5 Cut the tails at an angle or in points to finish off the bow.

WIRED LOOPS

1 To form a plain loop, cut a piece of ribbon and bring the cut ends together, right side out. Secure with wire to a floral pick.

2 To form a loop with a tail, use a longer ribbon. Cut the end of the tail into a "V" shape.

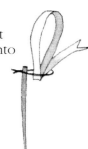

3 To make a loop with two tails, cut a length of ribbon twice as long as the first ribbon. Fold the ribbon in half with right sides out. Fold the doubled ribbons over again forming two tails. Pinch the ribbon together at these last folds and secure with wire to a floral pick. Trim ends as desired.

Create Your Own Decorations and Accessories

"E•Z Bowz" professional bow maker

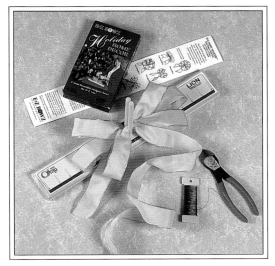

The E•Z Bow Maker™ comes with a full set of instructions so you can make professional bows every time. A video tape demonstrating this simple bow making tool may also be purchased.

The bow maker consists of a 2" wide, 18" long, wooden base with inches indicated on the top. Two holes for two 8" dowels, to be tapped into place with a hammer, hold the ribbon in place. It allows you to make perfect, beautiful bows from 2" to 16" wide.

The E•Z Bow Maker was designed to make bow making easy! You simply twist the ribbon, and insert it between the dowels. Then loop the ribbon back and forth across the top of the base. Make the loops as wide you wish and add as many loops as you want. Secure the center of the bow with floral wire, and fan out the loops on each side. Lift it from the base.

Purchase your E•Z Bow Maker at your local craft or fabric store or send $19.95 plus $3.50 shipping & handling for the bow maker and video to:
Mark Publishing, 5400 Scotts Valley Dr., Scotts Valley, CA 95066, Phone: (408)438-7668

Make sixteen exciting, different style bows for every occasion.

PINWHEEL BOW

CORSAGE BOW

TAILORED BOW

LAYERED BOW

MUM BOW

PIGGYBACK BOW

TUXEDO BOW

BUTTERFLY BOW

LAYERED BOW WITH TAILS

FLORAL BOW

WREATH BOW

TREE TOP BOW

SWAG BOW

PEW BOW

NESTED BOW

DOUBLE RIBBON BOW

CLASSIC GOLD

Materials

- 1 (Standard) bouquet holder
- 1 Bush (green) sword fern
- 2 Yards wired (gold) cording with tassels
- 2 (Gold filigree) 3" ornamental balls
- 6 Stems (white) calla lilies
- 2 Sprays (burgundy) grapes (2 clusters each)
- 5 Sprays (white) montelia (3 flowers each)

Tools:

- Wire cutters
- Yardstick
- Hot Glue
- Bouquet stand (See pg. 9)
- Floral wire, 22 gauge

1 Bouquet holder. Place the holder into the bouquet stand.

2 Sword fern. Cut all to 7".

Instructions:

3 Cord with tassel. Make two, 6" loops in the center of the cord. Bend the tails and cross them over each other.

4 Balls. Run a floral wire through the bottoms of each ball to make a "stem". Cut the wires to 3".

5 Calla lilies. Cut three to 7." Cut the others to 9", 10", and 16".

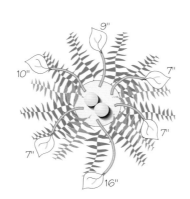

6 Grapes. Cut into four, 6" clusters. Cut the leaves to one 13" stem and four 6" stems.

7 Montelia. Cut into 7" stems.

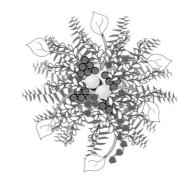

ENGLISH HANGING BALL

Materials

- 1 Round 3" Styrofoam ball
- 4 Yards (gold) cord
- 1 (Gold) 4" tassel
- 3 Sprays (green) sprengerii (3 stems each)
- 1 Stem (white) cymbidium orchid (14 blooms)
- 3 Sprays (white) cherry blossom (3 stems each)
- 2 Yards (gold) metallic ribbon size 9

Tools

- Floral wire, 18 gauge
- Wire cutters
- Yardstick
- Hot glue
- Scissors

1 Ball. Run a floral wire through the center of the ball. Make loops on the top and bottom.

Instructions

2 Cord and tassel. Hang the tassel from the bottom. Cut 4' of cord and fold in half. Tie the ends together onto the loop. With the other cord, make a loopy bow with 2" loops.

3 Sprengerii. Cut into 3½" sections.

4 Orchids. Cut apart leaving 4" of stem under each.

5 Cherry blossoms. Cut into 3½" sections, and fill in.

6 Ribbon. Cut the ribbon in half and make 2 loopy bows. Each has six, 2" loops. Glue them over the cord handle.

CANDLELIGHT ROMANCE

Materials

- 1 (Standard) bouquet holder
- 1 (Brass) 7" candlestick
- 1 Bush (variegated) dieffenbachia (16 leaves)
- 2 Sprays (green) sprengerii (3 stems each)
- 4 Stems (burgundy) parrot tulips
- 2 Sprays (cream) lilies (2 blooms each)
- 2 Sprays (cream) bridal berry (2 stems each)
- 3 Strands (gold) metal bullion
- 3 Yards (cream with gold edge) sheer ribbon size 100

Tools

- Wire cutters
- Hot glue

1 Bouquet holder and candlestick. Cut off the bouquet holder handle and glue it to the top of the candlestick.

Instructions

2 Dieffenbachia. Cut eight, 7" and eight, 4" leaves.

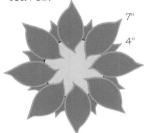

3 Sprengerii. Cut all to 3" and cover the foam.

4 Tulips. Cut all to 5".

5 Lilies. Cut all to 5". Add them around the tulips.

6 Bridal berries. Cut into 6" sections.

7 Gold bullion. Wrap one end around the stem of a tulip. Stretch it and weave it across the top of the flowers. Do the same with the others.

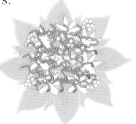

8 Ribbon. Make a loopy bow with four, 5" loops and 12" tails. Add an extra 17" tail.

Materials

- 1 (White) lace bouquet backing
- 1 (Standard) bouquet holder
- 1 Bush (green/white) caladium (6 leaves)
- 1 Bush (green) ivy (6 stems)
- 3 Stems (mauve) peony
- 3 Sprays (lavender) sweet peas (3 blooms each)
- 3 stems (cream) alstromeria (4 blooms each)

Tools:

- Bouquet stand
- Yardstick
- Wire cutters
- Hot glue

1 Lace backing and holder. Fit the lace backing onto the holder and place it into the stand.

2 Caladium and ivy. Cut all to 7". Make a circle around the back.

Instructions:

3 Peony. Cut all to 5".

4 Sweet peas. Cut all to 8". Cut the leaves and tendrils to 5" and fill in all over.

5 Alstromeria. Cut apart leaving a 3" stem under each. Fill in all over to cover the foam.

Garden Memories

Materials

- 5 Stems (white) calla lilies
- 2 Stems (white) sunflowers
- 4 Stems (white) freesia
- 1 Small bush (variegated) spider plant
- 2 Stems (green) sprengerii
- 2 Sprays (silver/burgundy) wandering Jew
- 2 Yards (sheer white) picot ribbon size 3
- 3 Yards (white) satin ribbon size 40
- 4 Yards (sheer white) pearl edged ribbon size 9

Tools:

- Wire cutters
- Yardstick
- Scissors
- Floral wire, 28 gauge
- Floral tape
- Hot glue

Instructions:

1 Calla lily. Cut to 26", 24", 23", 21" and 16". Wrap four with wire 10" up from the bottom.

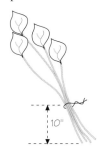

2 Sunflowers. Cut to 22" and 18". Lay them over the callas and wire them on. Wire the 16" calla over the sunflowers.

3 Freesia. Cut to 24", 23", 19" and 18". Stagger them through the flowers and wire them on.

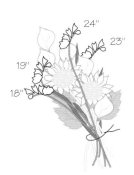

4 Spider plant and sprengerii. Cut the spider plant to 27" and 18". Add the long one to the back right side and the other one to the front left side of the bundle. Cut both sprengerii to 22". Wire all in place.

5 Wandering Jew. Cut to 18" and 22", and wire them in place. Tape over all the stems with floral tape, covering the bottom 11".

6 Ribbons. Tie a knot in the center of the picot ribbon. Place it at the base of the stems and criss-cross it up to the flowers. Using the satin ribbon, make a loopy bow with 10" tails and six, 6" loops. Glue it over the picot. Using the pearl edge ribbon, make another loopy bow with ten, 4" loops, two, 17" tails and an extra 15" hanging loop. Glue it to the satin ribbon bow.

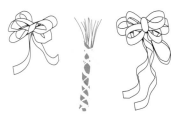

VICTORIAN DAYS

Materials

- 1 (White) lace fan
- 1 (Standard) bouquet holder
- 2 Stems (purple) open roses
- 4 Stems (lavender) star of Bethlehem
- 6 Stems (cream/purple) tulips
- 2 Sprays (white) ranunculi
- 1 Bush (green/white) caladium (12 leaves)
- 4 Yards (white) lace ribbon size 5

Tools

- Bouquet stand
- Wire cutters
- Hot glue
- Yardstick
- Floral wire, 22 gauge
- Scissors

Instructions

1 Fan and holder. Cut the fan handle to a 3" point. Insert it into the foam and add glue.

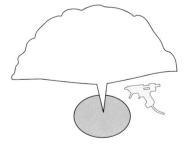

2 Roses. Cut both to 5".

3 Star of Bethlehem. Cut to 14", 10", 9" and 8".

4 Tulips. Cut three to 7" and three to 8". Add leaves behind the flowers.

5 Ranunculus. Cut two to 5", one to 6" and one to 7".

6 Caladium. Cut all to 5" and cover the back side.

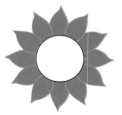

BACK VIEW SHOWING PLACEMENT OF GREENS

7 Ribbon. Make two, 3" and two, 6" single wired loops. Cut a 32" and a 36" length. Fold each in half and wire to the center. Add them as tails.

Materials

- 1 (White) lace parasol
- 1 6" Styrofoam ball
- 3 Sprays (purple) dendrobium orchids (2 stems each)
- 3 Stems (pink) open roses
- 3 Sprays (pink/green) foliage (3 stems each)
- 1 Spray (cream) carnations (3 stems each)
- 1 Yard (sheer white) picot ribbon size 3
- 1 Yard (white) mini pearl string
- 1 (white) satin ribbon flower

Tools

- Knife
- Hot glue
- Floral pins
- Corsage pins
- Wire cutters
- Yardstick
- Scissors
- Floral wire, 22 gauge

Instructions

1 Parasol and ball. Cut the ball in half. Holding the parasol with the handle up and the top collapsed, glue the ball back together over the stem of the handle so that it is hidden under the lace. Add floral pins to help keep the ball together. Fold the lace around the ball, securing it in place every 2" with a corsage pin.

2 Orchids. Cut one 18" three 15", one 12" and one 11".

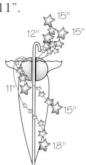

3 Roses. Cut to 8", 6" and 4". Glue rose leaves around each flower.

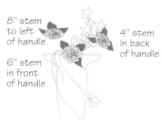

8" stem to left of handle

4" stem in back of handle

6" stem in front of handle

4 Foliage. Cut into 6" sections. Spread them out covering the foam.

5 Carnations. Cut all to 4". Fill in between the roses and foliage.

6 Ribbon, pearls and satin flower. Make a loopy bow with the ribbon with four, 3" loops and tails. Glue to the tip of the parasol. With the pearls, make single 2", 3" and 6" loops, and glue them to the bow. Glue the satin flower over the pearls.

PEACH DELIGHT

Materials

- 1 (Standard) bouquet holder
- 2 Stems (peach) open roses
- 5 Sprays (peach) lisianthus (2 stems each)
- 2 Sprays (cream) phalaenopsis orchid (2 stems each)
- 2 Sprays (green) foxtail (2 flowers each)
- 1 Bush (green) sword fern (5 stems each)
- 1 Spray (green/white) caladium (4 stems each)
- 1 Spray (gray) dusty miller (4 stems each)
- 3 Sprays (white) mini daisy (4 stems each)

Tools

- Bouquet stand
- Wire cutters
- Yardstick
- Hot glue

1 Bouquet holder and roses. Place the holder into the bouquet stand. Cut the roses to 7".

ALL ILLUSTRATIONS ARE TOP VIEW SHOWING PLACEMENT OF FLOWERS

Instructions

2 Lisianthus. Cut one to 4" and three to 7". Cut the others to 6", 8", 9", 11" and 13".

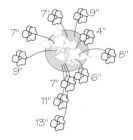

3 Orchids. Cut the stems to 11", 12", 13" and 17".

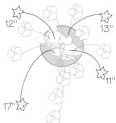

4 Foxtail. Cut the stems to 9", 10", 11" and 12".

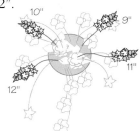

5 Sword fern. Cut the stems to 8", 9", 10", 10" and 13".

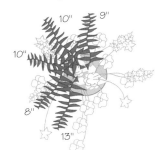

6 Caladium and dusty miller. Cut the caladium to 6", 7" and two to 8". Cut all the dusty miller to 9".

CALADIUM

DUSTY MILLER

7 Daisies. Cut one to 8" and the rest to 6". Fill in around the roses.

PRETTY IN PINK

Materials

 1 (Standard) bouquet holder

 4 Sprays (pink) rubrum lilies (3 flowers each)

 1 Bush (variegated) dieffenbachia (8 stems each)

 5 Sprays (pink) montelia (3 stems each)

 1 Bush (green) sprengerii (21 stems each)

Tools

 Bouquet stand

Wire cutters

Yardstick

 Hot glue

Instructions

1 Bouquet holder and lilies. Place the holder in the bouquet stand. Cut the medium blooms to 11", 8 ½", 6 ½" and 6". Cut the open blooms to 6 ½". Cut the small blooms to 7".

MEDIUM BLOOMS

OPEN BLOOMS
CUT ALL TO 6"

SMALL BLOOMS

2 Dieffenbachia. Cut one to 12" and the rest to 7".

3 Montelia. Cut two to 6 ½" and nine to 7 ½". Place them around the open lilies. Cut the others to 8", 8 ½", 9", 10" and 14". Cascade them from the bottom.

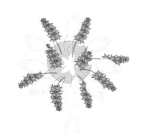

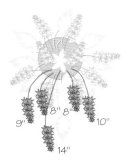

4 Sprengerii. Cut one 8", 7" and 6" stems. Add them to the bottom. Cut fifteen to 3 ½" and fill in. Cut three to 6" and cover the back.

Modern Traditions

Materials

- 1 (Standard) bouquet holder
- 5 Stems (white) 4" satin roses
- 3 Sprays (white) satin leaves (with pearls)
- 5 Stems (green) philodendron leaves
- 3 Sprays (green) plumosa (4 leaves each)

Tools

- Bouquet stand
- Wire cutters
- Yardstick
- Hot glue

Instructions

1 Bouquet holder and roses. Place the holder into the bouquet stand. Cut one rose to 4½", three to 6" and one to 13". Face all the flowers forward.

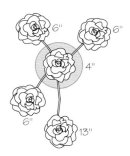

2 Leaves with pearls. Cut all to 9" and place them between the 6" flowers.

3 Philodendron. Cut all the leaves to 9".

4 Plumosa. Cut 1 spray to 11" and hang it at the bottom. Cut the others to 7" and fill in.

Materials

- 1 (Standard) bouquet holder
- 3 Stems (white) liatris
- 3 Stems (white) gerbera daisies
- 1 Bush (variegated) spider plant (12 stems each)
- 4 Sprays (white) oncidium orchids (3 stems each)
- 1 Bush (green) ivy (7 stems each)
- 1 Bush (variegated) dieffenbachia (5 stems each)

Tools

- Bouquet stand
- Wire cutters
- Yardstick
- Hot glue

1 Bouquet holder and liatris. Place the holder into the bouquet stand. Cut the liatris to 17", 9" and 8".

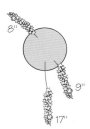

Instructions

2 Gerbera daisies. Cut two to 6" and one to 4". Face the bottom one forward.

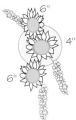

3 Spider plant. Cut two 6", six 7", three 10" and one 13" leaves. Cut a stem with baby plants to 14" and place it in the bottom. Wire together all the 7" leaves. Wrap two 10" leaves into a 5" loop and wire together.

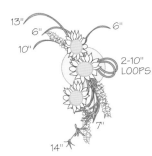

4 Orchids. Cut two 12", four, 8" and six, 6" stems.

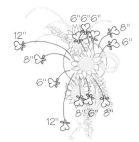

5 Ivy. Cut all to 3" and cover the foam.

6 Dieffenbachia. Cut all to 4".

Materials

- 1 (Standard) bouquet holder
- 1 Bush (variegated) dieffenbachia (7 stems each)
- 6 Stems (pink/cream) roses (2 open, 4 buds)
- 5 Stems (white) star of Bethlehem
- 3 Sprays (black/red) blackberry (2 stems each)
- 1 Bush (green) sword fern (5 stems each)
- 2 Sprays (green) maiden hair fern (2 stems each)
- 1 Spray (white) daisy (3 stems each)
- 3 Yards (white with pearls) sheer ribbon size 5

Tools

- Bouquet stand
- Wire cutters
- Yardstick
- Hot glue
- Scissors
- Floral wire, 22 gauge
- Wood picks with wire

Instructions

1 Bouquet holder and dieffenbachia. Place the holder into the bouquet stand. Cut all the leaves to 6".

2 Roses. Cut the open roses to 5½" and place them in the center. Cut two buds to 6", one to 6½" and one to 7½".

3 Star of Bethlehem. Cut three 8", one 11½" and one 14" stems.

4 Blackberry. Cut two 8" stems and the rest to 7", 11", 12" and 13".

5 Sword fern. Cut the stems to 4½", 6", 7", 10" and 13".

6 Daisies. Cut into 7", 6" and 5" stems. Place them around the center roses.

7 Maiden hair fern. Cut 10", 9", 7" and 6" stems.

8 Ribbon. Cut three, 12" strips and make 3 single 6" loops. Cut a 22" and 18" strip and wire each.

Blushing Bride

Materials

- 1 Stem (white) open rose
- 2 Stems (pink) open roses
- 2 Sprays (pink) magnolias (2 flowers each)
- 6 Stems (pink) rosebuds
- 4 Sprays (peach) bridal berries (2 stems each)
- 3 Sprays (green) sprengerii (2 stems each)
- 4 Sprays (white) stephanotis (3 stems each)
- 4 Yards (white) picot ribbon size 1
- 2 Yards (white) tulle

Tools

- Wire cutters
- Yardstick
- Hot glue
- Floral wire, 28 gauge
- Floral tape
- Scissors

Instructions

1 Cutting the flowers. Cut the white rose and all the rosebuds to 11". Cut all the pink open roses, magnolias and bridal berries to 10". Cut all the sprengerii and stephanotis to 8".

2 Assembling the flowers. Begin with the open white rose in your hand. Alternate the pink open roses and magnolias around it. Add the rosebuds and berry sprays between and around the other flowers. Alternate the sprengerii and stephanotis around the outside.

3 Ribbon. Bind the flower stems together by wrapping wire around them and taping over the wire with floral tape. Lay the center of the ribbon over the bottom of the stems and tie it in a knot. Crisscross the ribbon up the stem and tie it again at the base of the flowers.

4 Tulle. Cut the tulle into 3, 12" x 60" lengths. Make 3 loopy bows with 6, 4 ½" loops each. Glue them around the outside forming a collar.

Sweet Petal Basket

Materials

- 1 (White) 6" lace basket
- 4 Stems (pink) roses (2 open, 2 buds)
- 1 Bunch (green) small grapes
- Pink fresh roses or potpourri

Tools

- Yardstick
- Wire cutters
- Hot glue

Instructions

1. Basket and roses. Cut the stems off the open roses. Cut one bud to 5" and one to 2".

2. Grapes. Glue the grapes next to the open rose. Remove the leaves from the rose stems and fill in.

3. Rose petals or potpourri. Fill the basket with fresh, dry or silk petals for the flower girl to throw.

FLOWER GIRL'S DELIGHT

Materials

- 1 (White) 6" lace basket with foam insert
- 1 Bush (variegated) ivy (7 stems each)
- 3 Sprays (hot pink) roses (2 blooms, 1 bud each)
- 2 Sprays (pink) cherry blossom (2 stems each)
- 3 Sprays (white) oncidium orchids (4 stems each)
- 1 Bush (variegated) spider plant (12 stems each)

Tools

- Wire cutters
- Yardstick
- Hot glue

1 Basket and ivy. Cut one 4", five 7" and one 13" stems.

2 Roses. Cut all to 6".

3 Cherry blossom. Cut all to 5". Fill in around the basket.

4 Orchids. Cut all to 8".

5 Spider plant. Divide the plant into 3 sections and cut all to 8".

Ring of Posies

Materials

- 3 Sprays (white) mini daisies (3 stems each)
- 1 Spray (pink) cherry blossom (2 stems each)
- 3 Yards (white) picot ribbon size 1
- 1 Yard (pink) mini pearl garland

Tools

- Floral wire, 24 gauge
- Floral tape
- Wire cutters
- Yardstick
- Scissors

Instructions

1 Daisies and cherry blossoms. Cut all to 2". Measure the person's head and cut a wire to the correct length. Lay the flowers in an alternate pattern over the wire, taping each in place as you go. Once the wire is covered, bend it in a circle and wire the ends together.

2 Ribbon and pearls. Cut a 48" strip of ribbon and make a loopy bow with twelve 2" loops. Glue it to the back of the wreath. Make two, ½" loops with the pearls and glue them over the bow. Use the remaining ribbon and pearls to make tails and glue them under the bow.

Materials

Sweet Heart Ring Pillow

- 1 (White) heart shaped satin pillow
- 1 Spray (white) bouvardia (4 stems each)
- 1 Spray (white/pink) phalaenopsis orchid (2 blooms each)
- 2 Yards (white) picot ribbon size 1
- 2 Rings

Tools

- Wire cutters
- Yardstick
- Hot glue
- Scissors

Instructions

1. **Bouvardia.** Cut the spray to 10". Bend it and glue it across the pillow.

2. **Orchids.** Cut off the flower stems.

3. **Ribbon.** Cut the ribbon into 3 strips 26", 24" and 12" long. Knot the ribbons together near the tops and glue it to the pillow. Tie rings to ribbon.

Materials

Love Nest Ring Pillow

- 1 (Antique white) square satin pillow
- 2 Feet (cream) picot ribbon size 1
- 1 (Green) 3" round bird nest
- 2 Stems (pink) medium roses
- 1 Bunch (green) mini grapes
- 3 Sprays (white) stephanotis (8 blooms each)
- 2 Rings

Tools

- Wire cutters
- Scissors
- Yardstick
- Hot glue

Instructions

1. **Ribbon and Nest.** Tie a knot in the center of the ribbon. Glue it to the nest. Glue the nest to the pillow. Tie rings to ribbon.

2. **Roses.** Cut the flowers off the stem.

3. **Grapes.** Glue the cluster below the nest.

4. **Stephanotis.** Cut to 6", 4" and 3".

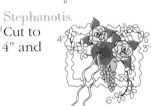

CROWNING GLORY

Materials

- 1 (White) pearl crown
- 1 (White) finger tip veil
- 4 Stems (white) cherry blossoms
- 1 (Clear) hair comb

Tools

- Hot glue
- Wire cutters
- Needle and thread

Instructions

1 **Crown and veil.** Center the veil on the wire band behind the crown and glue it in place. Secure it in place by wrapping thread around both.

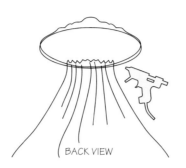

BACK VIEW

2 **Cherry blossoms and hair comb.** Cut the stems off the flowers and glue them over the top of the veil. Glue the comb to the inside of the veil just below the top and sew it in place by wrapping it with thread.

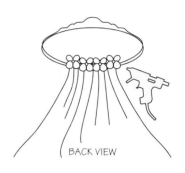

BACK VIEW

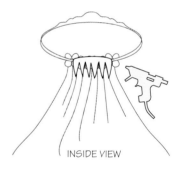

INSIDE VIEW

Materials

- 1 (White) satin head band
- 1 (White) finger tip veil
- 1 (Clear) hair comb
- 6 Sprays (white) satin orchids (with pearls)

Tools

- Hot glue
- Needle and thread
- Wire cutters

Instructions

1 Head band, veil and comb. Hot glue the top of the veil to the underside of the head band. Glue the comb to the veil. Secure the comb in place by wrapping it with thread.

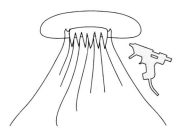

2 Orchids. Cut the stems off and glue them across the top of the head band end to end.

GREEK GODDESS

Materials

- 1 (White) double pearl band
- 1 (White) pearl flower spray
- 1 Yard (white) veil tulle with finished edge
- 1 (Clear) hair comb

Tools

- Floral wire, 28 gauge
- White floral tape
- Needle and thread
- Hot glue

Instructions

1 Band and pearl spray. Wire the pearl spray to the back of the band and tape it in place. Fit the band to the bride's head and wire and tape the back together.

2 Tulle. Make a rosette from the tulle. Wrap one end around in a tight circle and sew it in place. Keep wrapping the tulle around in circles and sew each circle to the previous one. Glue the rosette to the back of the pearl band.

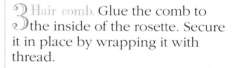

3 Hair comb. Glue the comb to the inside of the rosette. Secure it in place by wrapping it with thread.

SHY SWEETHEART

Materials

- 2 Stems (pink) open roses
- 3 Stems (pink) rosebuds
- 1 Spray (peach) bridal berries (2 stems each)
- 1 Hair barrette
- 1 Spray (white) stephanotis (3 stems each)
- 1 Spray (green) sprengerii (2 stems each)

Tools

- Wire cutters
- Yardstick
- Floral wire, 28 gauge
- Floral tape
- Hot glue

Instructions

1 Roses. Cut the open roses to 3". Cut two buds to 4" and one to 3". Wire and tape together one rose and one 4" bud. Do the same with the other bloom and two buds.

2 Bridal berries and barrette. Cut the berries to 3". Wire and tape 3 onto each rose cluster. Over lap the cluster stems and tape them together in the center forming a single spray. Glue it to the bar-rette.

3 Stephanotis and sprengerii. Cut the stephanotis from the stem and the sprengerii to 2". Glue them around the roses.

CORSAGES

Necklace Corsage

- 2 Blooms (white) phalaenopsis orchid
- 1 Spray (yellow) mini cosmos (3 stems each)
- ½ Yard (gold) wired cording
- 1 Stem (green/white) mini caladium
- 1 Yard (teal/gold) satin ribbon size 9

TOOLS

- Wire cutters
- Yardstick
- Floral tape
- Floral wire, 30 gauge
- Hot glue

INSTRUCTIONS

1 Orchids. Cut the stems to ½" and tape them together.

2 Cosmos. Cut two to 3" and tape them in place.

3 Cording. Take three, 1" loops and tape them to the bottom. Bend the tails around.

4 Caladium. Cut to 3" and glue it to the back. Do the same with two cosmos leaves.

5 Ribbon. Lay the corsage on the center of the ribbon and wire them together, and glue in place.

Wrist Corsage

- 1 Stem (white) open rose
- 1 Bloom (green) cymbidium orchid
- 1 Spray (cream) bridal berries (2 stems each)
- ½ Yard (gold) sheer ribbon size 9
- 1 Yard (gold/black) metallic ribbon size 9

Tools

- Wire cutters
- Yardstick
- Floral tape
- Floral wire, 30 gauge
- Hot glue

INSTRUCTIONS

1 Rose, orchid and berries. Cut the rose and orchid stems to 1". Cut the berries into two, 4" stems. Cluster all together and tape the stems.

2 Ribbon. Take three, 1½" loops with the sheer gold ribbon and add them to the bottom. Lay the corsage over the center of the other ribbon and wire it in place.

Shoulder Corsage

- 1 Spray (lavender) dendrobium orchid (2 stems each)
- 1 Spray (white) gardenia (4 blooms each)
- 3 Yards (burgundy) picot ribbon size 1
- 3 Corsage pins

Tools

- Wire cutters
- Yardstick
- Floral tape
- Floral wire, 30 gauge
- Hot glue

INSTRUCTIONS

1 Orchids. Cut one stem to 14". Bend it over a shoulder to find the balance point.

2 Gardenia. Cut all to 2" and glue in place. Glue leaves in the back.

3 Ribbon. Make 4 loopy bows. Make two with fourteen, 2" loops, one with eight, 1½" loops and the last with six, 1" loops. Cut three, 7" strips of ribbon.

Old Fashioned Rose

- 1 Stem (pink) open rose
- 1 Spray (lavender) alstromeria (4 blooms each)
- 1 Spray (white) stephanotis (5 blooms each)
- 1 Yard (sheer) gold edged ribbon size 5
- 2 Corsage pins

TOOLS

- Wire cutters
- Yardstick
- Floral tape
- Floral wire, 30 gauge
- Hot glue

INSTRUCTIONS

1 Rose and alstromeria. Cut the rose to 2". Cut the alstromeria to 2". Glue 3 alstromeria blooms around the rose.

2 Stephanotis. Cut all to 2". Glue them between the alstromeria. Glue rose leaves to the back.

3 Ribbon. Make a loopy bow with six, 2" loops and two, 4" tails.

Elegant Whites

- 1 Stem (white) sheer lily with leaves and pearls
- 1 Spray (green) plumosa (3 leaves each)
- 1 Leaf (green/white) caladium
- 2 Corsage pins

TOOLS

- Wire cutters
- Yardstick
- Floral tape

INSTRUCTIONS

1 Lilly. Cut the stem to 3" with leaves and pearls attached.

2 Plumosa. Cut all to 6".

3 Caladium. Cut the stem to 3" and tape it to the back.

Exotic Orchids

- 2 Blooms (white/pink) phalaenopsis orchid
- 1 Spray (pink) montelia (2 flowers each)
- 3 Leaves (green/white) caladium
- 1 Leaf (green) plumosa
- 2 Corsage pins

TOOLS

- Wire cutters
- Yardstick
- Floral tape
- Floral wire, 30 gauge
- Hot glue

INSTRUCTIONS

1 Orchid. Cut one to 5" and one to 3" and tape them together.

2 Montelia and caladium. Cut the montelia to 6" and 3". Tape them in place. Cut the caladium to 6", 4" and 3" and tape on.

3 Plumosa. Cut to 3" and glue it on.

Boutonnieres

A Rose is a Rose

- *2 Stems (pink) rosebuds*
- *1 Spray (white) stephanotis (5 blooms each)*
- *2 Leaves (variegated) ivy*
- *1 Leaf (green) plumosa*
- *1 Boutonniere pin*

Tools

- *Wire cutters*
- *Yardstick*
- *Floral tape*
- *Hot glue*

Instructions

1. Roses. Cut the stems to 5½" and 3". Tape them together.

2. Stephanotis. Cut all to 4" and tape in place.

3. Ivy and plumosa. Cut the stems off and glue in place.

Bold Exotics

- *1 Stem (white) calla lily bud*
- *1 Spray (purple) dendrobium orchid*
- *1 Stem (variegated) baby spider plant*
- *1 Stem (variegated) button foliage*
- *1 Boutonniere pin*

Tools

- *Wire cutters*
- *Yardstick*
- *Floral tape*
- *Hot glue*

Instructions

1. Calla lily and orchids. Cut the calla to 7". Cut the orchids to 5" and 2". Tape the orchids around the calla.

2. Spider plant and button foliage. Cut the spider plant to 2" and glue it to the front. Cut the button foliage to 5" and glue it on. Glue 2 orchid leaves to the back.

Traditional White

- *1 Spray (white) gardenia (2 blooms each)*
- *1 Spray (white) stephanotis (2 blooms each)*
- *1 Spray (green) sprengerii (3 stems each)*
- *1 Boutonniere pin*

Tools

- *Wire cutters*
- *Yardstick*
- *Floral tape*
- *Hot glue*

Instructions

1. Gardenia. Cut a bloom to 3" and a bud to 1". Tape them together.

2. Stephanotis. Cut to 4" and tape it in back.

3. Sprengerii. Cut three, 3" stems. Tape them on the left. Glue 2 gardenia leaves in back.

Modern White

- 2 Stems (white) satin roses
- 1 Spray (white) mini pearls with sequins
- 1 Leaf (green/white) caladium
- 1 Stem (variegated) button foliage
- 1 Boutonniere pin

TOOLS

- Wire cutters
- Yardstick
- Floral tape
- Hot glue

INSTRUCTIONS

1 Roses. Cut to 5" and 3½". Tape them together.

2 Pearls. Cut to 4" and tape on.

3 Caladium and button foliage. Cut the caladium to 4" and the button foliage to 3". Glue them on.

Satin Finish

- 1 Spray (white) satin orchid (with pearls)
- 1 Leaf (green) plumosa
- 1 Stem (variegated) baby spider plant
- 1 Boutonniere pin

TOOLS

- Wire cutters
- Yardstick
- Floral tape
- Hot glue

INSTRUCTIONS

1 Orchid and plumosa. Cut the orchid to 3". Cut the plumosa to 5" and tape them together.

2 Spider plant. Cut to 1" and glue to the front.

Simple Elegance

- 1 Spray (white) carnations (2 flowers each)
- 2 Leaves (variegated) ivy
- 1 Leaf (gray) dusty miller
- 1 Boutonniere pin

TOOLS

- Wire cutters
- Yardstick
- Floral tape
- Hot glue

INSTRUCTIONS

1 Carnations. Cut to 4" and 3" and tape them together.

2 Ivy and dusty miller. Cut off the ivy and cut the dusty miller to 4". Glue the dusty miller to the back and the ivy to the front.

CEREMONIAL KNEELING BENCH

Materials

- 1 Round 4" caged floral foam
- 1 Bush (variegated) dieffenbachia (10 stems each)
- 2 Stems (white) snapdragons
- 2 Stems (white) china mums
- 2 Bunches (green) medium grapes
- 2 Sprays (white) bouvardia (2 stems each)
- 2 Sprays (white) oncidium orchids (2 stems each)
- 2 Stems (green) onion grass

Tools

- Wire cutters
- Yardstick
- Hot glue
- Floral wire, 24 gauge

Instructions

1 Foam and dieffenbachia. Hang the foam on a chair. Cut the bush into one, 13", four, 7" and four, 6" stems.

2 Snapdragons. Cut to 15" and 11".

3 China mums and grapes. Cut the mums to 5" and 4". Make a wire stem for each grape bunch and add one below each mum.

4 Bouvardia. Cut one 9", two 8" and one 6" stems.

5 Orchids. Cut three 9" and one 6" stems.

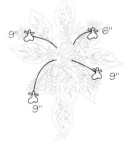

6 Onion grass. Cut the stem from the leaves. Divide the leaves in half from one stem and make 5" and 7" loops. Wire each. Divide the other leaves in half and wrap a wire around each.

Wedding Arch Top

Materials

- 1 Caged floral foam 5" x 7"
- 1 Branch (white) natural dogwood (2 stems each)
- 3 Stems (white) delphinium
- 4 Stems (white) snapdragons
- 4 Stems (white) calla lilies
- 2 Sprays (white) casa blanca lilies (3 flowers each)
- 3 Bunches (green) large grapes
- 2 (White) doves
- 1 Bush (green) sword fern (14 stems each)
- 1 Bush (variegated) dieffenbachia (8 stems each)
- 4 Stems (green) ivy vine
- 3 Yards (white) tulle
- 1 Bush (variegated) spider plant (9 leaves each)

Tools

- Floral wire, 16 and 24 gauge
- Wire cutters
- Yardstick
- Hot glue
- Scissors

ADDITIONAL PHOTO ON PAGE 49

Instructions

1. Foam. Hang the caged foam lengthwise on an arch or wall.

2. Dogwood. Lay the entire branch across the foam diagonally. Secure it in place with the 16 gauge wire and hot glue.

3. Delphinium. Cut two to 30" and one to 20".

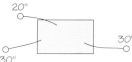

4. Snapdragons. Cut two 21", one 15" and one 13" stems.

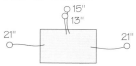

5. Calla lilies. Cut them to 21", 15", 13" and 11".

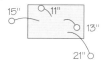

6. Casa blanca lilies. Cut two blooms to 9½". Cut the remaining sprays to 15".

7. Grapes. Make a wire stem for each grape cluster. Add them through the center to cover the foam.

8. Doves. Wire and glue the dove's feet to the dogwood branch.

9. Sword fern. Cut 2 stems each to 22", 21", 20", 16", 14", 13" and 12". Place the 22" stems behind the delphiniums on each side. Then graduate the stems up either side to the top.

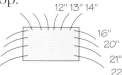

10. Dieffenbachia. Cut three 9", three 10", one 8" and one 11" stems.

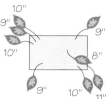

11. Ivy. Cut two 35" and two 25" stems.

12. Tulle. Cut a strip of tulle to 12" x 90". Cut another to 12" x 60". With the first strip make a loopy bow with 4, 8" loops and 2, 13" tails. Run the other strip through the center horizontally. Place the bow on the left and let the tails hang.

13. Spider plant. Cut 2 clusters of leaves to 16". Add baby plants to the clusters and let them hang.

Materials

(for each side)

- 1 Round 4" caged floral foam
- 1 Branch (white) natural dogwood (2 stems each)
- 1 Bush (green) sword fern (15 stems each)
- 3 Yards (white) tulle
- 2 Bunches (green) large grapes
- 1 Spray (white) casa blanca lily (3 flowers each)
- 7 Stems (green) trailing ivy
- 1 Stem (variegated) spider plant

Tools

- Wire cutters
- Yardstick
- Hot glue
- Floral wire, 24 and 16 gauge
- Scissors

(For the right side)

1 Foam and dogwood. Hang the foam to work on it. Lay the dogwood on top of the foam. Secure it in place with 16 gauge wire and hot glue.

Instructions

2 Sword fern. Cut eight 19", four 11" and a 16", 14" and 12" stems.

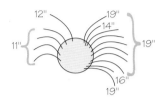

3 Tulle and grapes. Cut a strip of tulle to 24" x 82" and make a loopy bow with 2, 10" loops and a 26" and 16" tail. Make a wire stem for the grape clusters and hang them.

4 Casa blanca lilies. Bend the lily forward 3" under the blooms. Wire and glue the stem at the bend to the center of the foam. Allow it to hang.

5 Ivy. Cut to 18", 20" and 29". Wire the three together and glue them to the bottom. Cut four 8" stems and fill in the top.

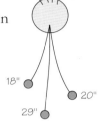

6 Spider plant. Cut to 10".

Note: To make the left side arrangement follow the same steps but reverse the placement of stems. Example: Step 2, instead of placing the 8, 19" stems on the right, place them on the left.

ADDITIONAL PHOTO ON PAGE 49

Unity of Love

Materials

- 1 Brick floral foam
- 1 (White) 3" x 10" pillar candle
- 1 Branch (burgundy) rose berry (2 stems each)
- 3 Stems (white) gerbera daisies
- 4 Stems (white) snapdragon
- 4 Stems (white) calla lilies
- 1 Bush (green) sword fern (10 stems each)
- 1 Bush (variegated) dieffenbachia (10 stems each)
- 4 Sprays (white) carnation (2 flowers each)
- 2 Bushes (red/green) prayer plant (6 stems each)
- Spanish moss

Tools

- Wire cutters
- Yardstick
- Floral pins
- Hot glue

Instructions

1. **Foam and candle.** Glue the candle to the right side of the foam. Surround the base of the candle with floral pins and then add more glue over the pins.

2. **Rose berry.** Cut into 24" stems. Curl one into a loop and cut to 13". Curl the end of the other until the length is 10".

3. **Gerbera daisies.** Cut to 9", 7" and 6".

4. **Snapdragons.** Cut to 18", 12", 10" and 10".

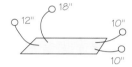

5. **Calla lilies.** Cut two 8", a 14" and 13" stems.

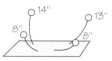

6. **Sword fern.** Cut six 10" and four 9" stems.

7. **Dieffenbachia.** Cut nine 8" and one 5" stems.

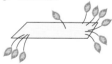

8. **Carnations and prayer plant.** Cut one carnation to 9", one to 7" and the rest to 2". Cover the foam with the 2". Cut the prayer plant into 4" stems and fill in.

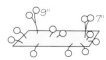

9. **Moss.** Cover any foam still showing with moss.

TRADITIONAL ALTAR ARRANGEMENTS

Materials

(For each arrangement)

- 1 Brick floral foam
- 1 (Brass) 6" round container
- 2 Stems (white) foxglove
- 1 Stem (brown) kiwi vine
- 2 Stems (white) giant mums
- 2 Sprays (white) Easter lilies (2 flowers each)
- 2 Sprays (white) pruna (2 stems each)
- 4 Stems (white) tulips
- 4 Sprays (white) mini daisy (2 Stems each)
- 1 Bush (variegated) dieffenbachia (10 Stems each)
- 1 Bush (variegated) spider plant (10 Stems each)
- 1 Spray (green) begonia vine (4 stems each)
- 1 Bunch (green) large grapes
- Spanish moss

Tools

- Wire cutters
- Yardstick
- Hot glue
- Floral pins
- Floral wire, 24 gauge
- Knife

Instructions

(For the right side arrangement)

1. Foam and container. Glue the foam into the container. Cut the foam to 2" above the edge of the container.

2. Foxglove and kiwi. Cut the foxglove to 29" and 25". Cut the kiwi vine into 11" and 25" sections.

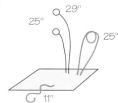

3. Mums. Cut to 10" and 11".

4. Easter lilies. Cut to 14" and 16".

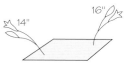

5. Pruna. Cut to 20" and 15".

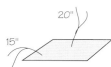

6. Tulips. Cut all to 15".

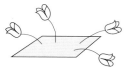

7. Daisies. Cut to 14", 12", 11" and 9". Spread out the flowers to fill in.

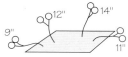

8. Dieffenbachia. Cut three, 12" leaves. Cut the remaining bush to 19".

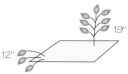

9. Spider plant. Separate the plant into 3 sections. Cut the sections to 19", 15" and 12".

10. Begonia vine and grapes. Cut the vine into 23", 13", 10" and 5" stems. Make a wire stem for the grapes and place them over the rim, in front.

Note: To make the arrangement for the left side, follow the same steps but reverse the placement sides of the stems. For example, in step 8 instead of adding the 3, 12" leaves to the lower left side, add them to the lower right side.

Materials
(for each)

- 1 Square 6" caged floral foam
- 1 Spray (green) philodendron vine (4 stems each)
- 3 Stems (white) delphinium
- 3 Stems (white) snapdragons
- 2 Stems (white) ball mums
- 1 Stem (white) phalaenopsis orchid
- 3 Sprays (white) freesia (2 flowers each)
- 2 Stems (white) tulips
- 3 Bunches (green) grapes
- 1 Bush (green) sword fern (6 stems each)
- 1 Bush (variegated) spider plant (20 stems and babies)

Tools

- Wire cutters
- Yardstick
- Hot glue
- Floral wire, 16 gauge

Instructions
(for both)

1 **Foam and philodendron.** Hang the foam to work on it. Cut two philodendron to 24" and two to 21".

2 **Delphinium.** Cut two to 25" and one to 22".

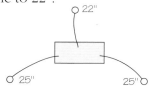

3 **Snapdragons.** Cut two to 21" and one to 11".

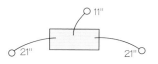

4 **Ball mums.** Cut to 11" and 9".

5 **Orchid and freesia.** Cut the orchid to 20". Cut the freesia to 20", 14" and 16".

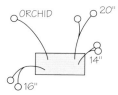

6 **Tulips.** Cut to 15" and 11".

7 **Grapes.** Make a wire stem for each bunch. Add them through the center of the foam to cover it.

8 **Sword fern.** Cut four 15" and two 8" stems.

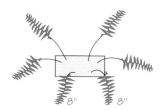

9 **Spider plant.** Divide the plant into 2 clusters. Add spider babies to hang.

ACCENTS OF GREEN

Materials

- *1(Standard) foam pew bow holder*
- *1 Stem (green/white) kale*
- *1 Bush (variegated) dieffenbachia (7 stems each)*
- *1 Bush (variegated) spider plant (15 stems)*
- *1 Bush (gray) dusty miller (10 stems each)*
- *2 Yards (white) tulle*

Tools

- *Wire cutters*
- *Yardstick*
- *Hot glue*
- *Floral wire, 24 gauge*
- *Scissors*

1 Foam and kale. Hang the holder on a chair to work on it. Cut the kale to 5".

2 Dieffenbachia. Cut four 7" and three 6" stems.

Instructions

3 Spider plant. Divide the plant into 3 clusters and add in. Bring 2 leaves from the top and glue them to 2 leaves from the bottom to make loops on the side.

4 Dusty miller. Cut all to 7".

5 Tulle. Make a loopy bow with four, 5" loops. Use the rest as the bow tails.

PINK PARADE

Materials

- 1 (Standard) foam pew bow holder
- 1 Bush (variegated) dieffenbachia (7 stems each)
- 1 Bush (variegated) mini ivy (6 stems each)
- 2 Sprays (green) plumosa (3 stems each)
- 1 Bush (gray) dusty miller (6 stems each)
- 3 Yards (white) wired satin ribbon size 4
- 1 Spray (Pink) rubrum lily (2 flowers, 3 buds)

Tools

- Wire cutters
- Yardstick
- Hot glue
- Floral wire, 24 gauge
- Scissors

1 Foam and dieffenbachia. Hang the holder on a chair to work on it. Cut all the dieffenbachia to 6½".

Instructions

2 Ivy. Cut all to 5".

3 Plumosa and dusty miller. Cut all to 8".

PLUMOSA   DUSTY MILLER

4 Ribbon. Make a floral bow with four, 4½" loops on the outside, two, 4" loops on the inside and two, 16" tails.

5 Rubrum lilies. Cut the blooms to 6" and 3". Cut two 8" and one 6" buds.

59

FLEMISH MASTERPIECE

Materials

- 2 Bricks floral foam
- 1 (White) 10" round container
- 4 Stems (pink) gladiolas
- 1 Branch (burgundy) rose berry (2 stems each)
- 3 Sprays (white) casa blanca lilies (3 flowers each)
- 3 Stems (yellow) pear branches
- 6 Stems (pink) parrot tulips
- 4 Sprays (green) sprengerii (2 stems each)
- 1 Bush (green) sword fern (13 stems)
- 1 Bush (green/pink) geranium vine (6 stems each)
- Spanish moss

Tools

- Wire cutters
- Yardstick
- Hot glue
- Floral pins
- Knife

Instructions

1. **Foam and container.** Glue the foam into the container. Cut the top to 2".

2. **Gladiolas.** Cut to 30", 28", 26" and 19".

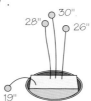

3. **Rose berry.** Cut one stem to 17". Bend the other around until the length is 21".

4. **Casa blanca lilies.** Cut to 28", 20" and 10".

5. **Pears and tulips.** Cut the pear branches to 22", 21" and 20". Cut one tulip to 20", three to 18", one to 16" and one to 12".

6. **Sprengerii.** Cut to 27", 26", 25" and 10"

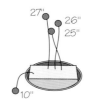

7. **Sword fern.** Cut nine to 15" and four to 9".

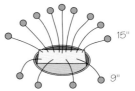

8. **Geranium vine and moss.** Cut the bush into 8" stems and fill in to cover the foam. Cover any remaining foam with moss. Secure with floral pins.

One Love, One Heart

Materials

- 1 (Mauve) 24" Styrofoam heart wreath
- 1 Brick floral foam
- 1 Piece 4" x 16" chicken wire
- 2 Branches (pink/cream) jumbo magnolia (2 stems each)
- 2 Stems (cream/pink) phalaenopsis orchid
- 3 Sprays (green) foxtail (2 flowers each)
- 1 Bush (variegated) spider plant (10 stems)
- 3 Yards (white) tull
- 2 (White) large doves

Tools

- Knife
- Wire cutters
- Floral pins
- Hot glue
- Floral wire, 18 gauge
- Yardstick
- Scissors

Instructions

1 Heart, foam and chicken wire. Cut the foam to 2½" wide x 4" long x 2" thick. Wrap the chicken wire around it and the heart. Add floral pins and hot glue. Make 2 hanging loops with the wire for the back.

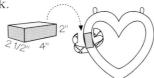

2 Magnolia. Measure 17" up one branch and 19" up the other. Cross the branches over at this point and wire them together. Cut the open blooms off with a 3" stem. Wire and glue the branches on top of the foam with the blooms over them.

3 Orchids. Cut to 19" and 18".

4 Foxtail. Cut a 19", 16", 15", 14" and two 13" stems.

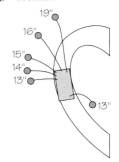
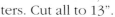

5 Spider plant. Make one, four leaf and two, three leaf clusters. Cut all to 13".

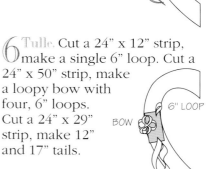

6 Tulle. Cut a 24" x 12" strip, make a single 6" loop. Cut a 24" x 50" strip, make a loopy bow with four, 6" loops. Cut a 24" x 29" strip, make 12" and 17" tails.

7 Birds. Cut the wire on the bird's feet to 1". Add glue and place them beak. Add dabs of glue over the feet and to the beaks.

Materials

(for a 3-layer cake)

- *1 (white) 6' daisy garland*
- *1 (green) 6" bird nest*
- *3 (Speckled) bird eggs*
- *3 Round 2" caged floral foam domes*
- *4 Bunches (green) small grapes*
- *3 Sprays (white) gardenia (3 flowers each)*
- *1 Spray (white) cymbidium orchid (14 flowers each)*
- *5 Sprays (white) oncidium orchids (3 stems each)*
- *5 Yards (white with gold edge) sheer wired ribbon size 40*

Tools

- *Floral wire, 24 gauge*
- *Wire cutters*
- *Floral tape*
- *Yardstick*
- *Scissors*
- *Wood picks with wire*
- *Hot glue*

1 Garland, nest and eggs. The garland is wrapped around the cake once it is set up. Glue the eggs in the nest.

2 Nest and flowers. You will need 1 bunch of grapes, 2 cymbidium flowers, 2 stems of an oncidium spray and 3 gardenia leaves.

Grapes. Cut off 2/3 of the bunch and glue it to the left. Glue the other to the top.

Cymbidiums. Cut the stems off and glue the flowers in place.

Oncidiums. Cut to 6" and glue to the nest.

Gardenia leaves. Frame in the flowers by gluing the leaves behind them.

3 Top layer of cake. You will need 1 caged foam, 1 spray of oncidiums, 2 gardenia flowers, 3 cymbidium flowers, 1 bunch of grapes and 2 yards of ribbon.

Foam and oncidiums. Cut the stems to 9", 7", and 6".

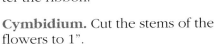

Gardenias. Cut to 1". Remove the leaves. Glue them in to cover the foam after the ribbon.

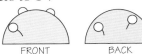

Cymbidium. Cut the stems of the flowers to 1".

FRONT   BACK

Grapes. Make a wire stem and glue it in.

Ribbon. Make a single 5 1/2" loop. Cut a 6" and 9" strip. Wire them together and add them as tails. Cut two 21" strips. Wire them on both ends and place one end in the foam.

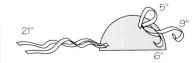

4 Middle layer of cake. You will need 1 caged foam, 4 stems of oncidium spray, 2 gardenia flowers, 3 cymbidium flowers, 1 bunch of grapes and 2 yards of ribbon.

Foam and oncidiums. Cut two 8", one 9" and one 10" stem.

Gardenias. Cut to 1". Remove the leaves. After the ribbon, glue them on to cover the foam.

Cymbidiums. Cut the stems of the flowers to 1".

Grapes. Make a wire stem and glue it in.

Ribbon. Make a single 5" loop. Cut two 27" strips and wire both ends together. Place one end into the foam.

5 Bottom layer of cake. You will need 1 caged foam, 6 stems of oncidium, 3 cymbidium flowers, 2 gardenias flowers, 1 bunch of grapes and 1 yard of ribbon.

Foam and oncidiums. Cut two 12" and four 10" stems.

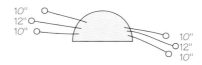

Cymbidiums. Cut the stem of each flower to 1".

Gardenias. Cut to 1". Remove the leaves. Glue them in to hide the foam after the ribbon.

Grapes. Make a wire stem and glue it in.

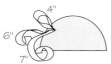

Ribbon. Make a single 4" loop. Cut a 6" and 7" strip. Wire the strips together at one end. Bend the other end to the desired shape.

6 Setting up the cake. Once the cake has been assembled in the desired location, you can set up the flowers. First, loop the garland around the bottom of the cake and fasten it together with wire. Then place the nest on top of it. Place the top layer arrangement on the right side, and the middle layer arrangement in the center. Place the bottom layer arrangement on the left. Connect all the arrangements together by placing the wired ends of the ribbon tails into the arrangement below it. Place the ribbon near the loops. *(See photo at right.)*

Rosy Favor Basket

Materials

- 1 (White) 14" oval basket with handle
- 1 Yard (white) tulle
- 5 Stems (pink) open roses
- 1 Bunch (green) medium grapes
- 7 Stems (pink) rosebuds
- 4 Sprays (white) mini gardenia (2 stems each)
- 4 Yards (white) pearl garland

Tools

- Wire cutters
- Scissors
- Yardstick
- Hot glue
- Floral wire, 26 gauge

Instructions

1 Tulle. Cut a strip 12" x 30". Glue it to the basket. Cut a strip to 12" x 40" and make a loopy bow with four, 5" loops. Glue it over the first strip. Cut six, 6" x 9" strips and make 6 small bows, with two, 3" loops.

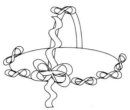

2 Open roses. Cut two 5", one 7" and two 4" stems and glue them in place.

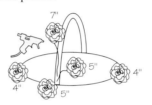

3 Grapes. Glue to the basket below the large bow.

4 Rosebuds. Cut all to 4". Remove the leaves and glue them in an alternating pattern every 2".

5 Gardenias. Cut into 3" stems.

6 Pearls. Cut into 3 equal sections. Glue one end of each into the center of the large bow.

Delicate Heart

- *1 (white) 9" round cut tulle*
- *1 Ounce (lavender) potpourri*
- *1 Yard (white) satin ribbon size ⅛"*
- *1 (white) 3" crochet heart*
- *1 Spray (white) satin rose and pearls*

TOOLS

- *Floral wire, 30 gauge*
- *Hot glue*
- *Wire cutters*

INSTRUCTIONS

1 Tulle and potpourri. Place a scoop of potpourri in the tulle. Wrap the tulle around it and wire the top.

2 Ribbon. Make a loopy bow with eight, 1" loops and two, 10" tails.

3 Heart and rose. Glue the potpourri to the heart. Cut the rose stem off and glue it to the bow.

Champagne Toast

- *1 (White) 9" round cut tulle*
- *1 Ounce (lavender) potpourri*
- *1 Yard (white) satin ribbon size ⅛"*
- *1 Stem (white) satin orchid*
- *2 Sprays (white) pearls*
- *1 (Clear) 3" champagne glass*

TOOLS

- *Floral wire, 30 gauge*
- *Hot glue*
- *Wire cutters*

INSTRUCTIONS

1 Tulle and potpourri. Place a scoop of potpourri in the tulle. Wrap the tulle around it and wire the top.

2 Ribbon. Make a loopy bow with six, 2" loops and two, 6" tails. Glue it on the tulle.

3 Orchid and pearls. Cut the orchid stem off and glue it to the bow. Cut the pearl spray stems to ½" and glue them behind the bow.

4 Champagne glass. Turn the glass over and glue the bottom of the potpourri to the base.

Elegant Fan

- *1 (white) 9" round cut tulle*
- *1 Ounce (lavender) potpourri*
- *1 Yard (white) satin ribbon size ⅛"*
- *1 Spray (white) satin rose with pearls*
- *1 (White) 3" crochet fan*

TOOLS

- *Floral wire, 30 gauge*
- *Hot glue*
- *Wire cutters*

INSTRUCTIONS

1 Tulle and potpourri. Place a scoop of potpourri in the tulle. Wrap the tulle around it, and wire the top.

2 Ribbon. Make a loopy bow with eight, 1" loops and two, 10" tails.

3 Rose. Cut off the stem and glue it to the bow.

4 Fan. Glue the potpourri to the fan.

Welcoming Cherub

Materials

- 1 Brick floral foam
- 1 (Black) standing cherub container (15" tall with a 6" dish)
- 1 Branch (burgundy) rose berry (2 stems each)
- 3 Stems (white) phalaenopsis orchids
- 1 (Green) 6" bird nest
- 7 Stems (white) star of Bethlehem
- 5 Stems (white) iris
- 5 Sprays (white) Easter lilies (3 flowers each)

Tools

- Knife
- Hot glue
- Wire cutters
- Yardstick

Instructions

1 Foam and container. Cut the foam to wedge it into the container with 2" above the rim.

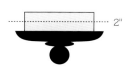

2 Rose berry. Cut the stems apart, 24" up from the bottom.

3 Orchids and bird nest. Cut two orchids to 36" and one to 6". Glue the 6" stem on the nest.

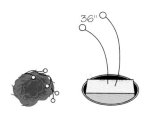

4 Star of Bethlehem. Cut one 20", and six, 13" stems.

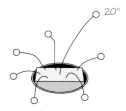

5 Iris. Cut all to 6" and spread them out evenly, filling in empty areas.

6 Easter lilies. Cut all to 6". Remove the leaves and glue them around each lily.

CIRCLE OF ETERNITY

Materials

- *3 Yards heavy gauge picture wire*
- *1 (Grapevine) 16" wreath*
- *1 (White) 6' daisy garland*
- *3 Stems (white) casa blanca lilies with buds*
- *3 Sprays (pink) roses (3 flowers each)*
- *6 Bunches (green) medium grapes*
- *1 Bush (green/white) caladium (20 stems each)*
- *4 Sprays (white) stephanotis (3 stems each)*
- *6 Yards (white with gold edge) sheer wired ribbon size 40*
- *2 Yards (white) satin ribbon size ⅛"*
- *6 (Fan and heart) wedding favors (See page 67)*

Tools

- *Yardstick*
- *Wire cutters*
- *Hot glue*
- *Scissors*
- *Floral wire, 24 gauge*

1 Picture wire and wreath. Cut three, 1 yard lengths of wire. Bend the top ends around in a loop. Attach the other ends to the wreath and glue in place. Hang the wreath to make sure it's level.

Instructions

2 Daisy garland. Wrap the garland around the wreath and wire in place.

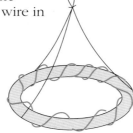

3 Casa blanca lilies. Cut all with a 1" stem.

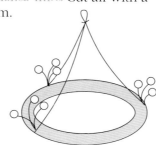

4 Roses. Cut apart with a 1" stem on each flower and a 3" stem on each bud. Remove the leaves and glue three around each rose.

5 Grapes. Glue a bunch to the lower left and to the right of each lily.

6 Caladium. Cut all to 3" and glue them in around the wreath filling in the empty spaces.

7 Stephanotis. Cut into 6" stems and glue them between the roses and lilies.

8 Thick ribbon. Make 3 loopy bows, each with three, 2½" loops, one 4" tail and one 12" tail. Glue them on each hanging wire 4" from the top. Glue the 4" tails up and the 12" tails down. Make a floral bow with 10 loops. The 6 outside loops are 3½" and the 4 inside loops are 3" with four, 6" tails.

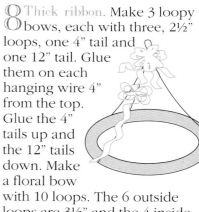

9 Thin ribbon and favors. Cut the ribbon into 10" sections. Tie a section onto each favor and hang them.

LOVE BIRDS

Materials

- *1 (Black) 10" x 16" bird cage*
- *1 Branch (burgundy) rose berry (2 stems)*
- *1 (Gray) 3" bird nest*
- *3 (Speckled) bird eggs*
- *1 (White) 3' mixed flower garland*
- *2 (White) large doves*
- *3 Yards (white with gold edge) sheer wired ribbon size 40*

Tools

- *Wire cutters*
- *Yardstick*
- *Hot glue*
- *Floral wire, 24 gauge*

1 Bird cage and rose berry. Bend the rose berry in circles and put it inside the cage.

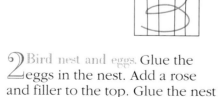

2 Bird nest and eggs. Glue the eggs in the nest. Add a rose and filler to the top. Glue the nest to the bottom of the cage.

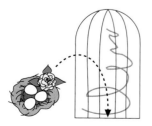

Instructions

3 Flower garland. Cut off ¼ of the garland and wire it to the top of the cage. Place the rest of the garland on the cage top and wire it in place.

BACK VIEW

4 Doves. Glue the doves to the front.

FRONT VIEW

5 Ribbon. Cut 12" and 36" lengths. Weave them through the garlands. Use the rest to make a loopy bow with four, 5" loops.

FLORAL THRONE

Materials

- 1 (white) 6' mixed flower garland
- 1 (white) 3' mixed flower garland
- 7 Yards (white with gold edge) sheer wired ribbon size 40
- 2 (Gold) 6' wired cords with tassels
- 1 Chair

Tools

- Yardstick
- Scissors
- Wire cutters
- Floral wire, 22 gauge

Instructions

1 Flower garlands, ribbon and cord. Cut four yards and two yards of ribbon. Weave the 4 yards through the 6' garland and the 2 yards through the 3' garland. Make a loopy bow with four, 5" loops. Make a loopy bow with a cord, with four, 6" loops and two, 12" tails.

2 Decorating the chair. Wire one end of the 6' garland to the left leg and wrap the ribbon bow around it. Wire one end of the 3' garland to the right leg. Place the other cord around the chair back and drape the ends through the garlands.

Materials

- 1 Sheet (white) 12" x 14" rice paper
- 1 (clear) 8" x 10" plastic box frame
- 1 Wedding invitation
- 1 (Antique gold) 8" x 10" wood frame
- 2 Yards (gold) cording
- 2 Sprays (lavender) bridal berries (2 stems each)
- 1 Spray (cream) lilies (2 flowers each)
- 4 Stems (pink) roses (1 open, 3 buds)
- 1 Spray (white) stephanotis (9 flowers each)
- 3 Yards (sheer) gold edged ribbon size 5

Tools

- Yardstick
- Scissors
- Double sided tape
- Hot glue
- Wire cutters
- Floral wire, 28 gauge

Instructions

1. Rice paper and box frame. Cut the corners out of the paper and fit it in the frame. Once fitted, tape it in place.

FOLD UP ON
DOTTED LINES

2. Invitation. Trim to 5" x 7". Tape it in 2" from the top.

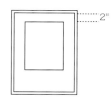

2"

3. Wood frame and cording. Glue the cording on the frame. Glue the wood frame onto the box frame.

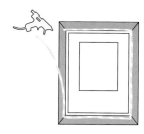

4. Bridal berries. Cut to 11" and 14" and glue in place.

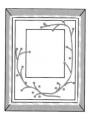

5. Lilies. Cut off the stems and glue on over the berries.

6. Roses. Cut off the stem of the open rose. Cut the buds with a 2" stem.

7. Stephanotis. Cut into four, 4" sections.

8. Ribbon. Make a loopy bow with eight, 1½" loops and 14" and 16" tails. Fill in empty areas with lily and rose leaves.